THIS JOURNAL BELONGS TO

_____

DATE

_____

Developed for busy lifestyles,

this journal has just enough room to capture five years' worth of goals, dreams, and accomplishments for every day of the year. When life comes at you from every direction, these inspiring quotes and Bible verses will remind you that, through it all, God has a plan...and it's good!

Our busy schedules don't always allow time for long journal entries. Yet there is always time for a line or two of gratitude or to record a memorable moment.

Start any time. Write the year in the space provided. Jot down a thought, a dream, a prayer. It is as easy as that. A simple note each day for five years will create a treasured collection of memories of how God has guided and provided along the way.

$\mathcal{F}$or I know the plans I have for you," declares the Lord, "plans to prosper you and not to harm you, plans to give you hope and a future."

JEREMIAH 29:11 NIV

20___ ....
....
....
....

20___ ....
....
....
....

20___ ....
....
....
....

20___ ....
....
....
....

20___ ....
....
....
....

Your future is as bright as the promises of God.

A. JUDSON

20 ___ ....
....
....
....

20 ___ ....
....
....
....

20 ___ ....
....
....
....

20 ___ ....
....
....
....

20 ___ ....
....
....
....

*G*od has a wonderful plan for each person.... He knew even before He created this world what beauty He would bring forth from our lives.

LOUISE B. WYLY

20___ ....
....
....
....

20___ ....
....
....

20___ ....
....
....

20___ ....
....
....

20___ ....
....
....

*L*ife is like an exciting book,
and every year starts a new chapter.

20 ___ ....
....
....
....

20 ___ ....
....
....
....

20 ___ ....
....
....
....

20 ___ ....
....
....
....

20 ___ ....
....
....
....

Don't follow the path. Go where there is no path and begin the trail. When you start a new trail equipped with courage, strength, and conviction, the only thing that can stop you is you!

RUBY BRIDGES

20___

....
....
....
....

20___

....
....
....
....

20___

....
....
....
....

20___

....
....
....
....

20___

....
....
....
....

God has designs on our future...and He has designed
us for the future. He has given us something to
do in the future that no one else can do.

RUTH SENTER

20___ ....
....
....
....

20___ ....
....
....
....

20___ ....
....
....
....

20___ ....
....
....
....

20___ ....
....
....
....

No eye has seen, no ear has heard, and no mind has imagined what God has prepared for those who love him.

1 CORINTHIANS 2:9 NLT

20 __ ....
....
....
....

20 __ ....
....
....
....

20 __ ....
....
....
....

20 __ ....
....
....
....

20 __ ....
....
....
....

*L*ife begins each morning.... Each morning is the open door to a new world—new vistas, new aims, new tryings.

LEIGH MITCHELL HODGES

20 __ ....
....
....
....

20 __ ....
....
....
....

20 __ ....
....
....
....

20 __ ....
....
....
....

20 __ ....
....
....
....

Nothing is as real as a dream.... Responsibilities need not erase it. Duties need not obscure it. Because the dream is within you, no one can take it away.

TOM CLANCY

20 __ ....
....
....
....

20 __ ....
....
....
....

20 __ ....
....
....
....

20 __ ....
....
....
....

20 __ ....
....
....
....

God created the universe, but He also created
you. God knows you, God loves you, and God
cares about the tiniest details of your life.

BRUCE BICKEL AND STAN JANTZ

20 ___ ....
....
....
....

20 ___ ....
....
....
....

20 ___ ....
....
....
....

20 ___ ....
....
....
....

20 ___ ....
....
....
....

*T*here are high spots in all of our lives, and most of them
come about through encouragement from someone else.

GEORGE ADAMS

20 _____ ....
....
....
....

20 _____ ....
....
....
....

20 _____ ....
....
....
....

20 _____ ....
....
....
....

20 _____ ....
....
....
....

If peace be in the heart, the wildest winter
storm is full of solemn beauty.

C. F. RICHARDSON

20 ___ ....
....
....
....

20 ___ ....
....
....
....

20 ___ ....
....
....
....

20 ___ ....
....
....
....

20 ___ ....
....
....
....

You are a creation of God unequaled anywhere in the universe. God never made anyone else exactly like you, and He never will again.

NORMAN VINCENT PEALE

20___ ....
....
....
....

20___ ....
....
....
....

20___ ....
....
....
....

20___ ....
....
....
....

20___ ....
....
....
....

*E*very good and perfect gift is from above, coming
down from the Father of the heavenly lights,
who does not change like shifting shadows.

JAMES 1:17 NIV

20___ ....
....
....
....

20___ ....
....
....
....

20___ ....
....
....
....

20___ ....
....
....

20___ ....
....
....
....

Heaven often seems distant and unknown,
but if He who made the road...is our guide,
we need not fear to lose the way.

HENRY VAN DYKE

20___ ....
....
....
....

20___ ....
....
....
....

20___ ....
....
....
....

20___ ....
....
....
....

20___ ....
....
....
....

The important thing really is not the deed
well done or the medal that you possess,
but the dedication and dreams out of which they grow.

ROBERT H. BENSON

20___

20___

20___

20___

20___

*G*od's love never ceases. Never.... God doesn't love us less
if we fail or more if we succeed. God's love never ceases.

MAX LUCADO

20 ___ ....
....
....

20 ___ ....
....
....

20 ___ ....
....
....

20 ___ ....
....
....

20 ___ ....
....
....

*A*mbition is the spur that makes a person
struggle with destiny. It is heaven's own incentive
to make purpose great and achievement greater.
DONALD G. MITCHELL

20 ___ ....
....
....
....

20 ___ ....
....
....
....

20 ___ ....
....
....
....

20 ___ ....
....
....
....

20 ___ ....
....
....
....

*There is surely a future hope for you,
and your hope will not be cut off.*

PROVERBS 23:18 NIV

20___ ....
....
....
....

20___ ....
....
....

20___ ....
....
....

20___ ....
....
....

20___ ....
....
....

*God makes a promise—faith believes it,
hope anticipates it, patience quietly awaits it.*

20___ ....
....
....
....

20___ ....
....
....
....

20___ ....
....
....
....

20___ ....
....
....
....

20___ ....
....
....
....

There is a loftier ambition than merely to stand high in the world. It is to stoop down and lift mankind a little higher.

HENRY VAN DYKE

20___ ....
....
....
....

20___ ....
....
....
....

20___ ....
....
....
....

20___ ....
....
....
....

20___ ....
....
....
....

*A*s white snow flakes fall quietly and thickly
on a winter day, answers to prayer will settle
down upon you at every step you take.

OLE HALLESBY

20__ ....
....
....
....

20__ ....
....
....
....

20__ ....
....
....
....

20__ ....
....
....
....

20__ ....
....
....
....

Wherever you are, be *all there*. Live to the hilt
every situation you believe to be the will of God.

JIM ELLIOT

20 ___

20 ___

20 ___

20 ___

20 ___

What happens when we live God's way? He brings
gifts into our lives...things like affection for others,
exuberance about life...and a conviction that
a basic holiness permeates things and people.

GALATIANS 5:22–23 MSG

20___ ....
....
....
....

20___ ....
....
....
....

20___ ....
....
....
....

20___ ....
....
....
....

20___ ....
....
....
....

Goals provide the energy source that powers our lives. One of the best ways we can get the most from the energy we have is to focus it. That is what goals can do for us—concentrate our energy.

DENIS WAITLEY

20 ___ ....
....
....
....

20 ___ ....
....
....
....

20 ___ ....
....
....
....

20 ___ ....
....
....
....

20 ___ ....
....
....
....

It is not the work we do that is so important.
It's the people we work with. It's the work
God does in our lives through them. And it's
the work He does in their lives through us.

KEN GIRE

20___

20___

20___

20___

20___

*I*n whatever ways that the Lord is blessing you...
recognize His winsome ways. He customizes
every dream He places in our hearts.

ROBIN JONES GUNN

20___ ....
....
....
....

20___ ....
....
....
....

20___ ....
....
....
....

20___ ....
....
....
....

20___ ....
....
....
....

Each one of us is God's special work of art. Through us, He teaches and inspires, delights and encourages, informs and uplifts all those who view our lives.

JONI EARECKSON TADA

20___ ....
....
....
....

20___ ....
....
....
....

20___ ....
....
....
....

20___ ....
....
....
....

20___ ....
....
....
....

Encourage one another and build up one another, just as you also are doing.

1 THESSALONIANS 5:11 NASB

20___

20___

20___

20___

20___

*H*ow could I be anything but quite happy if I believed always that all the past is forgiven, and all the present furnished with power, and all the future bright with hope.

JAMES SMETHAM

20 __ ....

....

....

....

20 __ ....

....

....

....

20 __ ....

....

....

....

20 __ ....

....

....

....

20 __ ....

....

....

....

*W*inter's snow transforms the woods into
a cathedral. Even the dark, drab hues of the woods
in early spring speak of hope and resurrection.

RAYMOND K. PETRUCCI

20 __ ....
....
....
....

20 __ ....
....
....
....

20 __ ....
....
....
....

20 __ ....
....
....
....

20 __ ....
....
....
....

We must start where we are and use what we have.
In the process of creation and relationship,
what seems mundane and trivial may show
itself to be holy, precious, part of a pattern.

LUCI SHAW

20 ___

....

....

....

....

20 ___

....

....

....

....

20 ___

....

....

....

....

20 ___

....

....

....

20 ___

....

....

....

....

Savor little glimpses of God's goodness
and His majesty, thankful for the gift of them.

WENDY MOORE

20____ ....
....
....
....

20____ ....
....
....
....

20____ ....
....
....
....

20____ ....
....
....
....

20____ ....
....
....
....

*L*et us not become weary in doing good, for at the proper
time we will reap a harvest if we do not give up. Therefore,
as we have opportunity, let us do good to all people.

GALATIANS 6:9–10 NIV

20___ ....
....
....
....

20___ ....
....
....
....

20___ ....
....
....
....

20___ ....
....
....
....

20___ ....
....
....
....

Beauty puts a face on God. When we gaze at nature, at a loved one, at a work of art, our soul immediately recognizes and is drawn to the face of God.

MARGARET BROWNLEY

20___ ....
....
....
....

20___ ....
....
....
....

20___ ....
....
....
....

20___ ....
....
....
....

20___ ....
....
....
....

Dedicate yourself to the call of your
heart and see where it leads you.

20___ ....
....
....
....

20___ ....
....
....
....

20___ ....
....
....
....

20___ ....
....
....
....

20___ ....
....
....
....

We may not all reach God's ideal for us, but with
His help we may move in that direction day by day
as we relate every detail of our lives to Him.

20___ ....
....
....
....

20___ ....
....
....
....

20___ ....
....
....
....

20___ ....
....
....
....

20___ ....
....
....
....

Whatever God tells us to do, He also helps us to do.
DORA GREENWELL

20___ ....
....
....
....

20___ ....
....
....
....

20___ ....
....
....
....

20___ ....
....
....
....

20___ ....
....
....
....

FEBRUARY 8

God promises to love me all day, sing songs
all through the night! My life is God's prayer.

PSALM 42:8 MSG

20___ ....
....
....
....

20___ ....
....
....
....

20___ ....
....
....
....

20___ ....
....
....
....

20___ ....
....
....
....

*It is necessary that we dream now and then.
No one ever achieved anything from the smallest
to the greatest unless the dream was dreamed first.*

LAURA INGALLS WILDER

20___ ....
....
....
....

20___ ....
....
....
....

20___ ....
....
....
....

20___ ....
....
....
....

20___ ....
....
....
....

*L*ife is not about discovering our talents;
it is about pushing our talents
to the limit and discovering our genius.
ROBERT BRAULT

20 ___ ....
....
....
....

20 ___ ....
....
....
....

20 ___ ....
....
....
....

20 ___ ....
....
....
....

20 ___ ....
....
....
....

*Every day we live is a priceless gift of God,
loaded with possibilities to learn something
new, to gain fresh insights.*

DALE EVANS ROGERS

20 __ ....
....
....
....

20 __ ....
....
....
....

20 __ ....
....
....
....

20 __ ....
....
....
....

20 __ ....
....
....
....

We are of such value to God that He came to live among us...and to guide us home. He will go to any length to seek us...to draw us back to Himself.

CATHERINE OF SIENA

20___ ....
....
....
....

20___ ....
....
....
....

20___ ....
....
....
....

20___ ....
....
....
....

20___ ....
....
....
....

*L*ove one another fervently with a pure heart.

1 PETER 1:22 NKJV

20＿

20＿

20＿

20＿

20＿

*L*ove is more than verses on valentines
and romance in the movies. Love is here and now,
real and true; the creator of our favorite memories
and the foundation of our fondest dreams.

20___ ....
....
....
....

20___ ....
....
....
....

20___ ....
....
....
....

20___ ....
....
....
....

20___ ....
....
....
....

$\mathcal{G}$od is the God of promise. He keeps His word, even when that seems impossible.

COLIN URQUHART

20___ ....
....
....
....

20___ ....
....
....
....

20___ ....
....
....
....

20___ ....
....
....
....

20___ ....
....
....
....

*I would rather walk with God
in the dark than go alone in the light.*

MARY GARDINER BRAINARD

20___ ....
....
....
....

20___ ....
....
....
....

20___ ....
....
....
....

20___ ....
....
....
....

20___ ....
....
....
....

*God may be invisible, but He's in touch. You may
not be able to see Him, but He is in control....
That includes all of life—past, present, future.*

CHARLES SWINDOLL

20___

....
....
....
....

20___

....
....
....

20___

....
....
....

20___

....
....
....

20___

....
....
....

*B*e careful how you live.... Make the most
of every opportunity.... Don't act thoughtlessly,
but understand what the Lord wants you to do.

EPHESIANS 5:15–17 NLT

20 ___ ....
....
....
....

20 ___ ....
....
....
....

20 ___ ....
....
....
....

20 ___ ....
....
....
....

20 ___ ....
....
....
....

For God's love is literally infinite. It is the shoreless sea
we are destined to swim in, surf in, and grow in forever.

PETER KREEFT

20___

20___

20___

20___

20___

*Inasmuch as anyone pushes you nearer
to God, he or she is your friend.*

20___ ....
....
....
....

20___ ....
....
....

20___ ....
....
....

20___ ....
....
....

20___ ....
....
....

$\mathcal{B}$e still, and in the quiet moments, listen to the voice
of your heavenly Father. His words can renew your
spirit.... No one knows you and your needs like He does.

JANET L. SMITH

20___ ....
....
....
....

20___ ....
....
....
....

20___ ....
....
....
....

20___ ....
....
....
....

20___ ....
....
....
....

Time is a very precious gift of God; so precious that it's only given to us moment by moment.

AMELIA BARR

20 __ ....
....
....
....

20 __ ....
....
....
....

20 __ ....
....
....
....

20 __ ....
....
....
....

20 __ ....
....
....
....

FEBRUARY 23

This is the day the LORD has made;
we will rejoice and be glad in it.

PSALM 118:24 NKJV

20___

20___

20___

20___

20___

God gives us dreams so we'll long for His reality.
BETH MOORE

20___ ....
....
....
....

20___ ....
....
....
....

20___ ....
....
....
....

20___ ....
....
....
....

20___ ....
....
....
....

*T*ry to keep your sense of humor!
When you can see the funny side of a problem,
sometimes it stops being so much of a problem.

EMILIE BARNES

20 ___

20 ___

20 ___

20 ___

20 ___

*I*magination is the beginning of creation.
You imagine what you desire, you will what you
imagine, and at last you create what you will.

GEORGE BERNARD SHAW

20 __ ....
....
....
....

20 __ ....
....
....
....

20 __ ....
....
....
....

20 __ ....
....
....
....

20 __ ....
....
....
....

It never hurts your eyesight to look
on the bright side of things.
BARBARA JOHNSON

20___ ....
....
....
....

20___ ....
....
....
....

20___ ....
....
....
....

20___ ....
....
....
....

20___ ....
....
....
....

Go after a life of love as if your life depended
on it—because it does. Give yourselves to the gifts
God gives you. Most of all, try to proclaim his truth.

1 CORINTHIANS 14:1 MSG

20___ ....
....
....
....

20___ ....
....
....
....

20___ ....
....
....
....

20___ ....
....
....
....

20___ ....
....
....
....

𝓕aith expects from God what is beyond all expectation.

ANDREW MURRAY

20___ ....
....
....
....

20___ ....
....
....
....

20___ ....
....
....
....

20___ ....
....
....
....

20___ ....
....
....
....

Gratitude unlocks the fullness of life. It turns what we
have into enough, and more.... It can turn a meal into
a feast, a house into a home, a stranger into a friend.

MELODY BEATTIE

20 ___ ....
....
....
....

20 ___ ....
....
....
....

20 ___ ....
....
....
....

20 ___ ....
....
....
....

20 ___ ....
....
....
....

*I*t is pleasing to God whenever you rejoice
or laugh from the bottom of your heart.

MARTIN LUTHER

20___ ....
....
....
....

20___ ....
....
....
....

20___ ....
....
....
....

20___ ....
....
....
....

20___ ....
....
....
....

*With God there is always more unfolding,
that what we can glimpse of the divine
is always exactly enough, and never enough.*

KATHLEEN NORRIS

20___

20___

20___

20___

20___

*D*on't judge each day by the harvest you reap
but by the seeds that you plant.
ROBERT LOUIS STEVENSON

20___ ....
....
....
....

20___ ....
....
....
....

20___ ....
....
....
....

20___ ....
....
....
....

20___ ....
....
....
....

*L*et everything you say be good and helpful, so that your words will be an encouragement to those who hear them.

EPHESIANS 4:29 NLT

20____ ....
....
....
....

20____ ....
....
....
....

20____ ....
....
....
....

20____ ....
....
....
....

20____ ....
....
....
....

No matter what our past may have held,
and no matter how many future days we have,
[God] stands beside us and loves us.

GARY SMALLEY AND JOHN TRENT

20___ ....
....
....
....

20___ ....
....
....
....

20___ ....
....
....
....

20___ ....
....
....
....

20___ ....
....
....
....

The true meaning of life is to plant trees under
whose shade you do not expect to sit.

NELSON HENDERSON

20___ ....
....
....
....

20___ ....
....
....
....

20___ ....
....
....
....

20___ ....
....
....
....

20___ ....
....
....
....

God is not an elusive dream or a phantom
to chase, but a divine person to know.
He does not avoid us, but seeks us.
When we seek Him, the contact is instantaneous.

NEVA COYLE

20___

20___

20___

20___

20___

Every breath we draw is a gift of His love,
every moment of existence is a gift of grace.

THOMAS MERTON

20____ ....
....
....
....

20____ ....
....
....
....

20____ ....
....
....
....

20____ ....
....
....
....

20____ ....
....
....
....

*L*et the wise listen and add to their learning,
and let the discerning get guidance.

PROVERBS 1:5 NIV

20___ ....
....
....
....

20___ ....
....
....
....

20___ ....
....
....
....

20___ ....
....
....
....

20___ ....
....
....
....

*A*ll that we have and are is one of the unique
and never-to-be repeated ways God has chosen
to express Himself in space and time.

BRENNAN MANNING

20 ___ ....
....
....
....

20 ___ ....
....
....
....

20 ___ ....
....
....
....

20 ___ ....
....
....
....

20 ___ ....
....
....
....

It's what you learn after you know it all that counts.
HARRY S. TRUMAN

20___ ....
....
....
....

20___ ....
....
....
....

20___ ....
....
....
....

20___ ....
....
....
....

20___ ....
....
....
....

When the world around us staggers from lack
of direction, God offers purpose, hope, and certainty.

GLORIA GAITHER

20___ ....

....

....

....

20___ ....

....

....

....

20___ ....

....

....

....

20___ ....

....

....

....

20___ ....

....

....

....

Ambition is that grit in the soul which creates disenchantment with the ordinary and puts the dare into dreams.

MAX LUCADO

20___ ....

....

....

....

20___ ....

....

....

....

20___ ....

....

....

....

20___ ....

....

....

....

20___ ....

....

....

....

*T*he ways of right-living people glow with light;
the longer they live, the brighter they shine.
PROVERBS 4:18 MSG

20 ___ ....
....
....
....

20 ___ ....
....
....
....

20 ___ ....
....
....
....

20 ___ ....
....
....
....

20 ___ ....
....
....
....

*G*od bless you and utterly satisfy your heart...with Himself.
AMY CARMICHAEL

20___ ....
....
....
....

20___ ....
....
....
....

20___ ....
....
....
....

20___ ....
....
....
....

20___ ....
....
....
....

You don't just luck into things as much as you'd like to think you do. You build them step by step, whether it's friendships or opportunities.

BARBARA BUSH

20___ ....

....

....

....

20___ ....

....

....

....

20___ ....

....

....

....

20___ ....

....

....

....

20___ ....

....

....

....

In God's wisdom, He frequently chooses
to meet our needs by showing His love toward
us through the hands and hearts of others.

JACK HAYFORD

20___ ....
....
....
....

20___ ....
....
....

20___ ....
....
....

20___ ....
....
....

20___ ....
....
....

The God who created, names, and numbers the stars
in the heavens also numbers the hairs of my head....
What matters to me matters to Him,
and that changes my life.

ELISABETH ELLIOT

20 ___ ....

....

....

....

20 ___ ....

....

....

....

20 ___ ....

....

....

....

20 ___ ....

....

....

....

20 ___ ....

....

....

....

*W*e know that in all things God works
for the good of those who love him,
who have been called according to his purpose.

ROMANS 8:28 NIV

20___ ....
....
....
....

20___ ....
....
....
....

20___ ....
....
....
....

20___ ....
....
....
....

20___ ....
....
....
....

$\mathcal{L}$ift up your eyes. Your heavenly Father waits
to bless you—in inconceivable ways to make your
life what you never dreamed it could be.

ANNE ORTLUND

20___ ....

....

....

....

20___ ....

....

....

....

20___ ....

....

....

....

20___ ....

....

....

....

20___ ....

....

....

....

MARCH 22

$\mathfrak{D}$on't be afraid to take a big step if one is indicated;
you can't cross a chasm in two small jumps.
DAVID LLOYD GEORGE

20 __ ....
....
....
....

20 __ ....
....
....
....

20 __ ....
....
....
....

20 __ ....
....
....
....

20 __ ....
....
....
....

Optimism is the faith that leads to achievement.
Nothing can be done without hope and confidence.

HELEN KELLER

20 __ ....
....
....
....

20 __ ....
....
....
....

20 __ ....
....
....
....

20 __ ....
....
....
....

20 __ ....
....
....
....

*B*egin today! No matter how feeble the light,
let it shine as best it may. The world may need
just that quality of light which you have.

HENRY C. BLINN

20 __ ....
....
....

20 __ ....
....
....

20 __ ....
....
....

20 __ ....
....
....

20 __ ....
....
....

May he give you the power to accomplish all the good things your faith prompts you to do.

2 THESSALONIANS 1:11 NLT

20___ ....
....
....
....

20___ ....
....
....
....

20___ ....
....
....
....

20___ ....
....
....
....

20___ ....
....
....
....

If we had no winter, the spring would
not be so pleasant: if we did not sometimes taste
of adversity, prosperity would not be so welcome.

ANNE BRADSTREET

20___

....

....

....

20___

....

....

....

20___

....

....

....

20___

....

....

....

20___

....

....

....

God is every moment totally aware of each one of us.
Totally aware in intense concentration and love....
No one passes through any area of life, happy
or tragic, without the attention of God with them.

EUGENIA PRICE

20___ ....

....

....

....

20___ ....

....

....

....

20___ ....

....

....

....

20___ ....

....

....

....

20___ ....

....

....

....

*G*o confidently in the direction of your
dreams. Live the life you have imagined.
HENRY DAVID THOREAU

20___ ....
....
....
....

20___ ....
....
....
....

20___ ....
....
....
....

20___ ....
....
....
....

20___ ....
....
....
....

Always be in a state of expectancy, and see that you
leave room for God to come in as He likes.

OSWALD CHAMBERS

20___ ....

....

....

....

20___ ....

....

....

....

20___ ....

....

....

....

20___ ....

....

....

....

20___ ....

....

....

....

MARCH 30

*Y*ou're blessed when you're content
with just who you are—no more, no less.
That's the moment you find yourselves proud
owners of everything that can't be bought.

MATTHEW 5:5 MSG

20___

....
....
....
....

20___

....
....
....
....

20___

....
....
....
....

20___

....
....
....
....

20___

....
....
....
....

You are God's created beauty and the
focus of His affection and delight.
JANET L. SMITH

20___ ....
....
....
....

20___ ....
....
....
....

20___ ....
....
....
....

20___ ....
....
....
....

20___ ....
....
....
....

Blue skies with white clouds.... Tulips and roses
and violets and dandelions and daisies.
Bluebirds and laughter and sunshine
and Easter. See how He loves us!

ALICE CHAPIN

20___ ....
....
....
....

20___ ....
....
....
....

20___ ....
....
....
....

20___ ....
....
....
....

20___ ....
....
....
....

*F*rom the tiny birds of the air and from the fragile
lilies of the field we learn the same truth...God takes care
of His own.... At just the right moment He steps
in and proves Himself as our faithful heavenly Father.

CHARLES SWINDOLL

20 ___ ....

....

....

....

20 ___ ....

....

....

....

20 ___ ....

....

....

....

20 ___ ....

....

....

....

20 ___ ....

....

....

....

The secret of life is that all we have
and are is a gift of grace to be shared.
LLOYD JOHN OGILVIE

20___

20___

20___

20___

20___

Give, and it will be given to you. A good measure,
pressed down, shaken together and running over,
will be poured into your lap. For with
the measure you use, it will be measured to you.

LUKE 6:38 NIV

20___ ....
....
....
....

20___ ....
....
....
....

20___ ....
....
....
....

20___ ....
....
....
....

20___ ....
....
....
....

How wonderful it is that nobody need wait a single
moment before starting to improve the world.

ANNE FRANK

20___ ....
....
....
....

20___ ....
....
....
....

20___ ....
....
....
....

20___ ....
....
....
....

20___ ....
....
....
....

*Our Lord has written the promise of the resurrection,
not in books alone, but in every leaf in springtime.*
MARTIN LUTHER

20___ ....
....
....
....

20___ ....
....
....
....

20___ ....
....
....
....

20___ ....
....
....
....

20___ ....
....
....
....

I believe that nothing that happens to me
is meaningless, and that it is good for us all that
it should be so.... As I see it, I'm here for some purpose.

DIETRICH BONHOEFFER

20___ ....
....
....
....

20___ ....
....
....
....

20___ ....
....
....
....

20___ ....
....
....
....

20___ ....
....
....
....

You learn something every day if you pay attention.
RAY LEBLOND

20___ ....
....
....
....

20___ ....
....
....
....

20___ ....
....
....
....

20___ ....
....
....
....

20___ ....
....
....
....

APRIL 9

Be content with who you are, and don't put on airs. God's strong hand is on you; he'll promote you at the right time. Live carefree before God; he is most careful with you.

1 PETER 5:7 MSG

20___ ....
....
....
....

20___ ....
....
....
....

20___ ....
....
....
....

20___ ....
....
....
....

20___ ....
....
....
....

To fall in love with God is the greatest of all
romances, to seek Him the greatest of all adventures,
to find Him the greatest human achievement.

AUGUSTINE

20___ ....
....
....
....

20___ ....
....
....
....

20___ ....
....
....
....

20___ ....
....
....
....

20___ ....
....
....
....

I marvel at the way
That hope keeps breaking through;
It is the Life in me
That keeps on reenacting...Resurrection.

GLORIA GAITHER

20___ ....
....
....
....

20___ ....
....
....
....

20___ ....
....
....
....

20___ ....
....
....
....

20___ ....
....
....
....

*L*ive today! Live fully each moment of today.
Trust God to let you work through this moment
and the next. He will give you all you need.

20 ___ ....
....
....
....

20 ___ ....
....
....
....

20 ___ ....
....
....
....

20 ___ ....
....
....
....

20 ___ ....
....
....
....

If you are seeking after God, you may be sure of this:
God is seeking you much more. He is the Lover,
and you are His beloved. He has promised Himself to you.

JOHN OF THE CROSS

20___

20___

20___

20___

20___

I will not forget you. See, I have inscribed
you on the palms of My hands.

ISAIAH 49:15–16 NKJV

20___ ....
....
....
....

20___ ....
....
....
....

20___ ....
....
....
....

20___ ....
....
....
....

20___ ....
....
....
....

The realities of faith, hope, and love can
make every day an exciting adventure.

NORMAN VINCENT PEALE

20___ ....
....
....
....

20___ ....
....
....
....

20___ ....
....
....
....

20___ ....
....
....
....

20___ ....
....
....
....

Easter is the demonstration of God that life is essentially spiritual and timeless.

CHARLES M. CROWE

20 —

20 —

20 —

20 —

20 —

*L*ive for today but hold your hands open
to tomorrow. Anticipate the future and its changes
with joy. There is a seed of God's love in every...
situation in which you may find yourself.

BARBARA JOHNSON

20___

20___

20___

20___

20___

The secret of joy in work is contained in one word—excellence. To know how to do something well is to enjoy it.

PEARL S. BUCK

20___ ....
....
....
....

20___ ....
....
....
....

20___ ....
....
....
....

20___ ....
....
....
....

20___ ....
....
....
....

God can do anything, you know—far more than you could ever imagine or guess or request in your wildest dreams!

EPHESIANS 3:20 MSG

20___

20___

20___

20___

20___

*G*od's promises are written on every leaf of springtime.

20 __

20 __

20 __

20 __

20 __

One hundred years from now it won't matter if you got
that big break, took the trip to Europe, or finally traded
up to a Mercedes.... It will matter that you knew God.

DAVID SHIBLEY

20___ ....
....
....
....

20___ ....
....
....
....

20___ ....
....
....
....

20___ ....
....
....
....

20___ ....
....
....
....

When you are inspired by a dream,
God has hit the ball into your court. Now you
have to hit it back with commitment.

ROBERT SCHULLER

20___ ....
....
....
....

20___ ....
....
....
....

20___ ....
....
....
....

20___ ....
....
....
....

20___ ....
....
....
....

APRIL 23

Spring bursts today,
For love is risen
and all the earth's at play.
CHRISTINA ROSSETTI

20__ ....

....

....

....

20__ ....

....

....

....

20__ ....

....

....

....

20__ ....

....

....

....

20__ ....

....

....

....

*T*rust in the LORD with all your heart,
and lean not on your own understanding; in all your
ways acknowledge Him, and He shall direct your paths.

PROVERBS 3:5-6 NKJV

20___ ....
....
....
....

20___ ....
....
....
....

20___ ....
....
....
....

20___ ....
....
....
....

20___ ....
....
....
....

God is the sunshine that warms us, the rain that
melts the frost and waters the young plants.
The presence of God is a climate of strong
and bracing love, always there.

JOAN ARNOLD

20 __ ....
....
....
....

20 __ ....
....
....
....

20 __ ....
....
....
....

20 __ ....
....
....
....

20 __ ....
....
....
....

We are so preciously loved by God that we cannot even comprehend it. No created being can ever know how much and how sweetly and tenderly God loves them.

JULIAN OF NORWICH

20___ ....
....
....
....

20___ ....
....
....
....

20___ ....
....
....
....

20___ ....
....
....
....

20___ ....
....
....
....

APRIL 27

In difficulties, I can drink freely of God's power
and experience His touch of refreshment and blessing—
much like an invigorating early spring rain.

ANABEL GILLHAM

20___

_____

_____

_____

20___

_____

_____

_____

20___

_____

_____

_____

20___

_____

_____

_____

20___

_____

_____

_____

*We are made to persist. That's how
we find out who we are.*

TOBIAS WOLFF

20___ ....
....
....
....

20___ ....
....
....
....

20___ ....
....
....
....

20___ ....
....
....
....

20___ ....
....
....
....

*P*ursue a righteous life—a life of wonder, faith, love,
steadiness, courtesy. Run hard and fast in the faith.
Seize the eternal life, the life you were called to.

1 TIMOTHY 6:11–12 MSG

20__ ....
....
....
....

20__ ....
....
....
....

20__ ....
....
....
....

20__ ....
....
....
....

20__ ....
....
....
....

Some blessings—like rainbows after rain
or a friend's listening ear—are extraordinary gifts
waiting to be discovered in an ordinary day.
TINA MARIE SCHUHRKE

20___ ....
....
....
....

20___ ....
....
....
....

20___ ....
....
....
....

20___ ....
....
....
....

20___ ....
....
....
....

MAY 1

Spring has arrived. Everywhere we look
the process of transformation from death to life
is seen. New life is bursting forth all about us.

RAYMOND K. PETRUCCI

20 ___ ....
....
....
....

20 ___ ....
....
....
....

20 ___ ....
....
....
....

20 ___ ....
....
....
....

20 ___ ....
....
....
....

All who have accomplished great things have had a great aim, have fixed their gaze on a goal which was high, one which sometimes seemed impossible.
ORISON SWETT MARDEN

20___ ....

....

....

....

20___ ....

....

....

....

20___ ....

....

....

....

20___ ....

....

....

....

20___ ....

....

....

....

Each day comes bearing gifts. Untie the ribbons.
RUTH ANN SCHABACKER

20___ ....
....
....

20___ ....
....
....

20___ ....
....
....

20___ ....
....
....

20___ ....
....
....

If God cares so wonderfully for wildflowers
that are here today and thrown into the fire
tomorrow, he will certainly care for you.

MATTHEW 6:30 NLT

20 _____ ....
....
....
....

20 _____ ....
....
....
....

20 _____ ....
....
....
....

20 _____ ....
....
....
....

20 _____ ....
....
....
....

When we dream alone, it remains only a dream.
When we dream together, it is not just a
dream. It is the beginning of reality.

HÉLDER CÂMARA

20___

20___

20___

20___

20___

Spring had come once more...lingering along through
April and May in a succession of sweet, fresh, chilly days,
with pink sunsets and miracles of resurrection and growth.

LUCY MAUD MONTGOMERY

20___ ....
....
....
....

20___ ....
....
....
....

20___ ....
....
....
....

20___ ....
....
....
....

20___ ....
....
....
....

This day is all that is good and fair.
It is too dear, with its hopes and invitations,
to waste a moment on yesterdays.

RALPH WALDO EMERSON

20__ ....
....
....
....

20__ ....
....
....
....

20__ ....
....
....
....

20__ ....
....
....
....

20__ ....
....
....
....

God loves us for ourselves. He values our love more
than He values galaxies of new created worlds.

A. W. TOZER

20___ ....
....
....
....

20___ ....
....
....
....

20___ ....
....
....
....

20___ ....
....
....
....

20___ ....
....
....
....

May the God of hope fill you with all joy and peace
as you trust in him, so that you may overflow with hope.

ROMANS 15:13 NIV

20___ ....
....
....
....

20___ ....
....
....
....

20___ ....
....
....
....

20___ ....
....
....
....

20___ ....
....
....
....

No one can fully measure the blessings that come
to the life of the one who has a praying mother.

Roy Lessin

20___ ....

....

....

....

20___ ....

....

....

....

20___ ....

....

....

....

20___ ....

....

....

....

20___ ....

....

....

....

Hope is the ability to hear the music of the future....
Faith is having the courage to dance to it today.

PETER KUZMIČ

20___ ....
....
....
....

20___ ....
....
....
....

20___ ....
....
....
....

20___ ....
....
....
....

20___ ....
....
....
....

Wise are those who learn that the bottom line
doesn't always have to be their top priority.

WILLIAM A. WARD

20___ ....

....

....

....

20___ ....

....

....

....

20___ ....

....

....

....

20___ ....

....

....

....

20___ ....

....

....

....

*All that I am or hope to be, I owe to my angel mother.
My mother's prayers...have clung to me all my life.*

ABRAHAM LINCOLN

20___

....

....

....

20___

....

....

....

20___

....

....

....

20___

....

....

....

20___

....

....

....

*D*on't fuss about what's on the table...or if the clothes
in your closet are in fashion. There is far more
to your inner life.... Look at the ravens...carefree
in the care of God. And you count far more.

LUKE 12:22–24 MSG

20 ___ ....

....

....

....

20 ___ ....

....

....

....

20 ___ ....

....

....

....

20 ___ ....

....

....

....

20 ___ ....

....

....

....

*W*hen we allow God the privilege of shaping our lives, we discover new depths of purpose and meaning. What a joyful thought to realize you are a chosen vessel for God—perfectly suited for His use.

JONI EARECKSON TADA

20___ ....
....
....
....

20___ ....
....
....
....

20___ ....
....
....
....

20___ ....
....
....
....

20___ ....
....
....
....

If I can thank God for the good of the past,
I can trust Him for the good of the future, no matter
what lies down that road. I can walk the planks—
from known to unknown—and know: He holds.

ANN VOSKAMP

20 __ ....
....
....
....

20 __ ....
....
....
....

20 __ ....
....
....
....

20 __ ....
....
....
....

20 __ ....
....
....
....

What we feel, think, and do this moment influences both
our present and the future in ways we may never know.

ALEXANDRA STODDARD

20 ___ ....

....

....

....

20 ___ ....

....

....

....

20 ___ ....

....

....

....

20 ___ ....

....

....

....

20 ___ ....

....

....

....

*Things turn out best for the people who make
the best out of the way things turn out.*
ART LINKLETTER

20 __ ....
....
....
....

20 __ ....
....
....
....

20 __ ....
....
....
....

20 __ ....
....
....
....

20 __ ....
....
....
....

*I*t was God...who made the garden grow in your hearts.

1 CORINTHIANS 3:6 TLB

20___

....
....
....

20___

....
....
....

20___

....
....
....

20___

....
....
....

20___

....
....
....

God's love is like a river springing up...and
flowing endlessly through His creation, filling all
things with life and goodness and strength.

THOMAS MERTON

20 ___ ....
....
....
....

20 ___ ....
....
....
....

20 ___ ....
....
....
....

20 ___ ....
....
....
....

20 ___ ....
....
....
....

The measure of a life, after all,
is not its duration but its donation.

CORRIE TEN BOOM

20___ ....
....
....
....

20___ ....
....
....
....

20___ ....
....
....
....

20___ ....
....
....
....

20___ ....
....
....
....

MAY 22

God came to us because God wanted to join us
on the road, to listen to our story, and to help
us realize that we are not walking in circles
but moving toward the house of peace and joy.

HENRI J. M. NOUWEN

20___ ....
....
....
....

20___ ....
....
....
....

20___ ....
....
....
....

20___ ....
....
....
....

20___ ....
....
....
....

Don't ever let yourself get so busy that you
miss those little but important extras in life—
the beauty of a day...the smile of a friend.

20____

20____

20____

20____

20____

What a wonderful God we have—
he is...the source of every mercy, and the one who
so wonderfully comforts and strengthens us.

2 CORINTHIANS 1:3-4 TLB

20___ ....
....
....
....

20___ ....
....
....
....

20___ ....
....
....
....

20___ ....
....
....
....

20___ ....
....
....
....

God knows everything about us. And He cares
about everything. Moreover, He can manage
every situation. And He loves us! Surely this
is enough to open the wellsprings of joy.

HANNAH WHITALL SMITH

20___ ....
....
....
....

20___ ....
....
....
....

20___ ....
....
....
....

20___ ....
....
....
....

20___ ....
....
....
....

*Always do your best. What you plant
now, you will harvest later.*

OG MANDINO

20___

....
....
....
....

20___

....
....
....
....

20___

....
....
....
....

20___

....
....
....
....

20___

....
....
....
....

We have a Father in heaven who is almighty,
who loves His children...and whose very joy
and delight it is to...help them at all times.
GEORGE MUELLER

20___

20___

20___

20___

20___

*L*ovely flowers are the smiles of God's goodness.

<small>WILBERFORCE</small>

20___

20___

20___

20___

20___

MAY 29

Steep yourself in God-reality,
God-initiative, God-provisions. You'll find
all your everyday human concerns will be met.

LUKE 12:30 MSG

20___

20___

20___

20___

20___

*T*aken separately, the experiences of life
can work harm and not good. Taken together,
they make a pattern of blessing and strength
the like of which the world does not know.

V. RAYMOND EDMAN

20___ ....
....
....
....

20___ ....
....
....
....

20___ ....
....
....
....

20___ ....
....
....
....

20___ ....
....
....
....

If we all did the things we are capable of doing,
we would literally astound ourselves.

THOMAS EDISON

20___ ....
....
....
....

20___ ....
....
....
....

20___ ....
....
....
....

20___ ....
....
....
....

20___ ....
....
....
....

The patterns of our days are always changing...
rearranging...and each design for living is
unique...graced with its own special beauty.

20___ ....
....
....
....

20___ ....
....
....
....

20___ ....
....
....
....

20___ ....
....
....
....

20___ ....
....
....
....

God created us with an overwhelming desire
to soar.... He designed us..."to mount up with
wings like eagles," realistically dreaming of
what He can do with our potential.

CAROL KENT

20 __ ....
....
....
....

20 __ ....
....
....
....

20 __ ....
....
....
....

20 __ ....
....
....
....

20 __ ....
....
....
....

JUNE 3

*The steadfast love of the LORD never ceases,
his mercies never come to an end; they are new
every morning; great is your faithfulness.*

LAMENTATIONS 3:22–23 NRSV

20___

20___

20___

20___

20___

*F*aith is deliberate confidence in the character of God
whose ways you may not understand at the time.

OSWALD CHAMBERS

20___ ....
....
....
....

20___ ....
....
....
....

20___ ....
....
....
....

20___ ....
....
....
....

20___ ....
....
....
....

JUNE 5

*The same God...who directs the earth in its orbit,
who feeds the burning furnace of the sun, and keeps
the stars perpetually burning with their fires—
the same God has promised to supply your strength.*

CHARLES SPURGEON

20___ ....
....
....
....

20___ ....
....
....
....

20___ ....
....
....
....

20___ ....
....
....
....

20___ ....
....
....
....

I am convinced beyond a shadow of any
doubt that the most valuable pursuit
we can embark upon is to know God.

KAY ARTHUR

20___ ....
....
....
....

20___ ....
....
....
....

20___ ....
....
....
....

20___ ....
....
....
....

20___ ....
....
....
....

JUNE 7

Happiness is living by inner purpose,
not by outer pressures.
DAVID AUGSBURGER

20___ ....
....
....
....

20___ ....
....
....
....

20___ ....
....
....
....

20___ ....
....
....
....

20___ ....
....
....
....

JUNE 8

*Oh, how sweet the light of day, and how
wonderful to live in the sunshine! Even if you live
a long time, don't take a single day for granted.
Take delight in each light-filled hour.*

ECCLESIASTES 11:7–8 MSG

20 _____ ....

....

....

....

20 _____ ....

....

....

20 _____ ....

....

....

20 _____ ....

....

....

20 _____ ....

....

....

....

JUNE 9

Everyone has a unique role to fill in the world and is important in some respect. Everyone, including and perhaps especially you, is indispensable.

NATHANIEL HAWTHORNE

20 ___

20 ___

20 ___

20 ___

20 ___

JUNE 10

What we are is God's gift to us.
What we become is our gift to God.

ELEANOR POWELL

20 ___ ....

....

....

....

20 ___ ....

....

....

....

20 ___ ....

....

....

....

20 ___ ....

....

....

....

20 ___ ....

....

....

....

We are not called by God to extraordinary things,
but to do ordinary things with extraordinary love.

JEAN VANIER

20 ___ ....
....
....
....

20 ___ ....
....
....
....

20 ___ ....
....
....
....

20 ___ ....
....
....
....

20 ___ ....
....
....
....

*It is difficult to say what is impossible,
for the dream of yesterday is the hope
of today and the reality of tomorrow.*
ROBERT H. GODDARD

20___

20___

20___

20___

20___

Clothe yourselves with compassion, kindness, humility,
gentleness and patience.... Forgive as the Lord
forgave you. And over all these virtues put on love,
which binds them all together in perfect unity.

COLOSSIANS 3:12–14 NIV

20___ ....
....
....
....

20___ ....
....
....
....

20___ ....
....
....
....

20___ ....
....
....
....

20___ ....
....
....
....

JUNE 14

Friends are an indispensable part of a meaningful life.
BEVERLY LAHAYE

20___ ....
....
....
....

20___ ....
....
....
....

20___ ....
....
....
....

20___ ....
....
....
....

20___ ....
....
....
....

JUNE 15

*There is much satisfaction in work well done,
but there can be no happiness equal to the
joy of finding a heart that understands.*

VICTOR ROBINSON

20＿ ....
....
....
....

20＿ ....
....
....
....

20＿ ....
....
....
....

20＿ ....
....
....
....

20＿ ....
....
....
....

JUNE 16

Thank You, Lord, for fathers. They give us glimpses of who we are, where we came from, and the possibilities of what we can be.

BARBARA FARMER

20___ ....
....
....
....

20___ ....
....
....
....

20___ ....
....
....
....

20___ ....
....
....
....

20___ ....
....
....
....

I don't know what the future holds,
but I know who holds the future.

E. STANLEY JONES

20___ ....
....
....
....

20___ ....
....
....
....

20___ ....
....
....
....

20___ ....
....
....
....

20___ ....
....
....
....

Where you are right now is God's place for you.
Live and obey and love and believe right there.

1 CORINTHIANS 7:17 MSG

20___ ....
....
....
....

20___ ....
....
....
....

20___ ....
....
....
....

20___ ....
....
....
....

20___ ....
....
....
....

God's timing is rarely our timing. But far better
than we do, He numbers our days and knows our
moments and our hours. Our task is to trust.

OS GUINNESS

20 ___ ....
....
....
....

20 ___ ....
....
....
....

20 ___ ....
....
....
....

20 ___ ....
....
....
....

20 ___ ....
....
....
....

Do well the little things now; and then great things
will come to you by and by, asking to be done.

PERSIAN PROVERB

20 __ ....

....

....

....

20 __ ....

....

....

....

20 __ ....

....

....

....

20 __ ....

....

....

....

20 __ ....

....

....

....

JUNE 21

*Like the summer breezes playing,
like the tall trees softly swaying,
like the lips of silent praying
is the perfect peace of God.*

MICHAEL PERRY

20___ ....
....
....
....

20___ ....
....
....
....

20___ ....
....
....
....

20___ ....
....
....
....

20___ ....
....
....
....

JUNE 22

You can't experience success beyond your wildest dreams until you dare to dream something wild!
SCOTT SORRELL

20__ ....
....
....
....

20__ ....
....
....
....

20__ ....
....
....
....

20__ ....
....
....
....

20__ ....
....
....
....

See what great love the Father has lavished on us,
that we should be called children
of God! And that is what we are!

1 JOHN 3:1 NIV

20___

20___

20___

20___

20___

JUNE 24

*L*et God have you, and let God love you—
and don't be surprised if your heart begins
to hear music you've never heard and your
feet learn to dance as never before.

MAX LUCADO

20___ ....

....

....

....

20___ ....

....

....

....

20___ ....

....

....

....

20___ ....

....

....

....

20___ ....

....

....

....

JUNE 25

*In this world it is not what we take up,
but what we give up that makes us rich.*
HENRY WARD BEECHER

20___ ....
....
....
....

20___ ....
....
....
....

20___ ....
....
....
....

20___ ....
....
....
....

20___ ....
....
....
....

God knows the rhythm of my spirit and knows my heart thoughts. He is as close as breathing.

20 ___

20 ___

20 ___

20 ___

20 ___

JUNE 27

*God specializes in things fresh and firsthand....
His plans for you this year may outshine
those of the past.... He's prepared to fill your
days with reasons to give Him praise.*

JONI EARECKSON TADA

20 __ ....
....
....
....

20 __ ....
....
....
....

20 __ ....
....
....
....

20 __ ....
....
....
....

20 __ ....
....
....
....

JUNE 28

*L*ive out your God-created identity.
Live generously and graciously toward
others, the way God lives toward you.

MATTHEW 5:48 MSG

20___ ....
....
....
....

20___ ....
....
....
....

20___ ....
....
....
....

20___ ....
....
....
....

20___ ....
....
....
....

What lies behind us and what lies before us are tiny matters compared to what lies within us.

HENRY STANLEY HASKINS

20___

....
....
....
....

20___

....
....
....

20___

....
....
....

20___

....
....
....

20___

....
....
....

God...does not distribute Himself that each may
have a part, but to each one He gives all
of Himself as fully as if there were no others.

A. W. TOZER

20 __ ....
....
....
....

20 __ ....
....
....
....

20 __ ....
....
....
....

20 __ ....
....
....
....

20 __ ....
....
....
....

It's morning again, little hope, and the world's drying off with fresh-laundered sunshine. Life's face is never the same though we may look at it for all eternity.

KOLBEIN FALKEID

20___ ....
....
....
....

20___ ....
....
....
....

20___ ....
....
....
....

20___ ....
....
....
....

20___ ....
....
....
....

May God give you eyes to see beauty
only the heart can understand.

20___ ....
....
....
....

20___ ....
....
....

20___ ....
....
....

20___ ....
....
....

20___ ....
....
....

JULY 3

$\mathcal{T}$he Lord will guide you always;
he will satisfy your needs in a sun-scorched land....
You will be like a well-watered garden,
like a spring whose waters never fail.

ISAIAH 58:11 NIV

20___ ....
....
....
....

20___ ....
....
....
....

20___ ....
....
....
....

20___ ....
....
....
....

20___ ....
....
....
....

JULY 4

*Real freedom comes only with the experience
and practice of authentic love.*

EUGENIA PRICE

20___ ....
....
....
....

20___ ....
....
....
....

20___ ....
....
....
....

20___ ....
....
....

20___ ....
....
....
....

Enthusiasm is a kind of faith that has been set on fire.
GEORGE M. ADAMS

20 ___ ....
....
....
....

20 ___ ....
....
....
....

20 ___ ....
....
....
....

20 ___ ....
....
....
....

20 ___ ....
....
....
....

If God hath made this world so fair...
How beautiful beyond compare
Will paradise be found!
JAMES MONTGOMERY

20 ___

20 ___

20 ___

20 ___

20 ___

Stretch out your hand and receive the world's
wide gift of joy, appreciation, and beauty.
CORINNE ROOSEVELT ROBINSON

20 __ ....

20 __ ....

20 __ ....

20 __ ....

20 __ ....

JULY 8

*H*ow precious it is, Lord, to realize that you are
thinking about me constantly! I can't even count how
many times a day your thoughts turn towards me.

PSALM 139:17–18 TLB

20___ ....
....
....
....

20___ ....
....
....
....

20___ ....
....
....
....

20___ ....
....
....
....

20___ ....
....
....
....

JULY 9

Our Creator would never have made such lovely days,
and given us the deep hearts to enjoy them,
above and beyond all thought,
unless we were meant to be immortal.

NATHANIEL HAWTHORNE

20___

....

....

....

....

20___

....

....

....

....

20___

....

....

....

....

20___

....

....

....

....

20___

....

....

....

....

*E*xperience God in the breathless wonder
and startling beauty that is all around you.
WENDY MOORE

20___ ....
....
....
....

20___ ....
....
....
....

20___ ....
....
....
....

20___ ....
....
....
....

20___ ....
....
....
....

It is not how much we have,
but how much we enjoy,
that makes happiness.
CHARLES H. SPURGEON

20___ ....

....

....

....

20___ ....

....

....

....

20___ ....

....

....

....

20___ ....

....

....

....

20___ ....

....

....

....

*A*ll that is good, all that is true,
all that is beautiful, all that is beneficent,
be it great or small...comes from God.

JOHN HENRY NEWMAN

20___ ....

....

....

....

20___ ....

....

....

....

20___ ....

....

....

....

20___ ....

....

....

....

20___ ....

....

....

....

*Y*ou created my inmost being; you knit me together in my mother's womb. I praise you because I am fearfully and wonderfully made.

PSALM 139:13–14 NIV

20___ ....
....
....
....

20___ ....
....
....
....

20___ ....
....
....
....

20___ ....
....
....
....

20___ ....
....
....
....

Nature decrees that we do not exceed the speed of light. All other impossibilities are optional.

ROBERT BRAULT

20__ ....
....
....
....

20__ ....
....
....
....

20__ ....
....
....
....

20__ ....
....
....
....

20__ ....
....
....
....

*We all mold one another's dreams.
We all hold each other's fragile hopes in our
hands. We all touch others' hearts.*

20__ ....
....
....
....

20__ ....
....
....
....

20__ ....
....
....
....

20__ ....
....
....
....

20__ ....
....
....
....

*Our God is so wonderfully good, and lovely,
and blessed in every way that the mere fact of belonging
to Him is enough for an untellable fullness of joy!*

HANNAH WHITALL SMITH

20___ ....
....
....
....

20___ ....
....
....
....

20___ ....
....
....
....

20___ ....
....
....
....

20___ ....
....
....
....

Optimists are nostalgic about the future.

20___ ....
....
....
....

20___ ....
....
....

20___ ....
....
....

20___ ....
....
....

20___ ....
....
....
....

O LORD my God...your plans for us are too numerous
to list.... If I tried to recite all your wonderful
deeds, I would never come to the end of them.

PSALM 40:5 NLT

20___ ....
....
....
....

20___ ....
....
....
....

20___ ....
....
....
....

20___ ....
....
....
....

20___ ....
....
....
....

That is God's call to us—simply to be people who
are content to live close to Him and to renew the kind
of life in which the closeness is felt and experienced.

THOMAS MERTON

20____ ....
....
....
....

20____ ....
....
....
....

20____ ....
....
....
....

20____ ....
....
....
....

20____ ....
....
....
....

$\mathcal{F}$aith in God gives your life a center from which
you can reach out and dare to love the world.

BARBARA FARMER

20___ ....
....
....
....

20___ ....
....
....
....

20___ ....
....
....
....

20___ ....
....
....

20___ ....
....
....
....

*Gratitude makes sense of our past, brings peace
for today, and creates a vision for tomorrow.*

MELODY BEATTIE

20___ ....
....
....
....

20___ ....
....
....
....

20___ ....
....
....
....

20___ ....
....
....
....

20___ ....
....
....
....

God has a purpose for your life and no
one else can take your place.

20___ ....
....
....
....

20___ ....
....
....
....

20___ ....
....
....
....

20___ ....
....
....
....

20___ ....
....
....
....

The LORD longs to be gracious to you; therefore
he will rise up to show you compassion....
Blessed are all who wait for him!

ISAIAH 30:18 NIV

20__ ....
....
....
....

20__ ....
....
....
....

20__ ....
....
....
....

20__ ....
....
....
....

20__ ....
....
....
....

*B*efore anything else, above all else, beyond everything else, God loves us. God loves us extravagantly, ridiculously, without limit or condition. God is in love with us.

ROBERTA BONDI

20___ ....
....
....
....

20___ ....
....
....
....

20___ ....
....
....
....

20___ ....
....
....
....

20___ ....
....
....
....

JULY 25

The way the golden sunlight streaks through
the lush greens and browns of a summer
wood is nothing short of divine.

RAYMOND K. PETRUCCI

20 ___ ....

....

....

....

20 ___ ....

....

....

....

20 ___ ....

....

....

....

20 ___ ....

....

....

....

20 ___ ....

....

....

....

In those times I can't seem to find God, I rest
in the assurance He knows how to find me.

NEVA COYLE

20___ ....
....
....
....

20___ ....
....
....

20___ ....
....
....

20___ ....
....
....

20___ ....
....
....

*A*llow your dreams a place in your prayers
and plans. God-given dreams can help you move
into the future He is preparing for you.

BARBARA JOHNSON

20___ ....

....

....

....

20___ ....

....

....

....

20___ ....

....

....

....

20___ ....

....

....

....

20___ ....

....

....

....

May you have the power to understand...how wide,
how long, how high, and how deep his love is.

EPHESIANS 3:17 NLT

20____

20____

20____

20____

20____

God's heart is the most sensitive
and tender of all. No act goes unnoticed,
no matter how insignificant or small.

RICHARD J. FOSTER

20 ___ ....
....
....
....

20 ___ ....
....
....
....

20 ___ ....
....
....
....

20 ___ ....
....
....
....

20 ___ ....
....
....
....

You are not here merely to make a living.
You are here in order to enable the world
to live more amply, with greater vision,
with a finer spirit of hope and achievement.

WOODROW WILSON

20 _____

20 _____

20 _____

20 _____

20 _____

Every person's life is a fairy tale written by God's fingers.
HANS CHRISTIAN ANDERSEN

20___ ....
....
....
....

20___ ....
....
....
....

20___ ....
....
....
....

20___ ....
....
....
....

20___ ....
....
....
....

AUGUST 1

There will always be the unknown.
There will always be the unprovable.
But faith confronts those frontiers with a thrilling
leap. Then life becomes vibrant with adventure!

ROBERT SCHULLER

20___ ....
....
....
....

20___ ....
....
....
....

20___ ....
....
....
....

20___ ....
....
....
....

20___ ....
....
....
....

Nothing in all creation will ever be able to separate us from the love of God.

ROMANS 8:39 NLT

20___

....
....
....
....

20___

....
....
....
....

20___

....
....
....
....

20___

....
....
....
....

20___

....
....
....
....

God will use whatever we commit to
Him to bring good into our lives.
GLORIA GAITHER

20＿

20＿

20＿

20＿

20＿

God wants us to approach life, full of expectancy that God is going to be at work in every situation as we grow in our faith in Him.

COLIN URQUHART

20___ ....
....
....
....

20___ ....
....
....
....

20___ ....
....
....
....

20___ ....
....
....
....

20___ ....
....
....
....

When nothing is sure, everything is possible.
LIBBIE FUDIM

20___

20___

20___

20___

20___

AUGUST 6

What makes life worthwhile is having a big
enough objective, something which catches our
imagination and lays hold of our allegiance....
What higher...goal can there be than to know God?

J. I. PACKER

20___ ....
....
....
....

20___ ....
....
....
....

20___ ....
....
....
....

20___ ....
....
....
....

20___ ....
....
....
....

Those who hope in the LORD will renew their strength.
They will soar on wings like eagles; they will run and
not grow weary, they will walk and not be faint.

ISAIAH 40:31 NIV

20 ___ ....
....
....
....

20 ___ ....
....
....

20 ___ ....
....
....

20 ___ ....
....
....

20 ___ ....
....
....
....

*R*eal joy comes not from ease or riches
or from the praise of people,
but from doing something worthwhile.

WILFRED GRENFELL

20___ ....
....
....
....

20___ ....
....
....
....

20___ ....
....
....
....

20___ ....
....
....
....

20___ ....
....
....
....

*H*ope is not a dream, but a way
of making dreams become reality.
L. J. SUENENS

20___ ....
....
....

20___ ....
....
....

20___ ....
....
....

20___ ....
....
....

20___ ....
....
....

*T*hose who build the future are those who know that greater things are yet to come, and that they themselves will help bring them about.

MELVIN J. EVANS

20 ___

20 ___

20 ___

20 ___

20 ___

Know that you yourself are a miracle.

NORMAN VINCENT PEALE

20___

20___

20___

20___

20___

O LORD, you have examined my heart and know
everything about me.... You go before me and follow
me. You place your hand of blessing on my head.

PSALM 139:1, 5 NLT

20 ___ ....
....
....
....

20 ___ ....
....
....
....

20 ___ ....
....
....
....

20 ___ ....
....
....
....

20 ___ ....
....
....
....

When seeds of kindness are sown prayerfully
in the garden plot of our lives, we may
be sure that there will be a bountiful harvest
of blessings for both us and others.

W. PHILLIP KELLER

20___ ....
....
....
....

20___ ....
....
....
....

20___ ....
....
....
....

20___ ....
....
....
....

20___ ....
....
....
....

Our inner happiness depends not on what we experience but on the degree of our gratitude to God, whatever the experience.

ALBERT SCHWEITZER

20 ___ ....
....
....
....

20 ___ ....
....
....
....

20 ___ ....
....
....
....

20 ___ ....
....
....
....

20 ___ ....
....
....
....

God's friendship is the unexpected joy we find
when we reach for His outstretched hand.

JANET L. SMITH

20___ ....
....
....
....

20___ ....
....
....
....

20___ ....
....
....
....

20___ ....
....
....
....

20___ ....
....
....
....

*Incredible as it may seem, God wants our
companionship.... He wants to be a father
to us, to shield us, to protect us, to counsel us,
and to guide us in our way through life.*

BILLY GRAHAM

20___ ....

....

....

....

20___ ....

....

....

....

20___ ....

....

....

....

20___ ....

....

....

....

20___ ....

....

....

....

The LORD will...watch over your life; the LORD will watch over your coming and going both now and forevermore.

PSALM 121:7–8 NIV

20 ___ ....
....
....
....

20 ___ ....
....
....
....

20 ___ ....
....
....
....

20 ___ ....
....
....
....

20 ___ ....
....
....
....

God wants you to know Him as personally as He knows you. He craves a genuine relationship with you.

TOM RICHARDS

20___ ....
....
....
....

20___ ....
....
....
....

20___ ....
....
....
....

20___ ....
....
....
....

20___ ....
....
....
....

Our truest life is when we are in dreams awake.
HENRY DAVID THOREAU

20___

....

....

....

20___

....

....

....

20___

....

....

....

20___

....

....

....

20___

....

....

....

*I'm a little pencil in the hands of a loving God
who is writing a love letter to the world.*

MOTHER TERESA

20___ ....
....
....
....

20___ ....
....
....
....

20___ ....
....
....
....

20___ ....
....
....
....

20___ ....
....
....
....

He made you so you could share in His creation,
could love and laugh and know Him.

TED GRIFFEN

20___

20___

20___

20___

20___

AUGUST 22

*Y*our eyes are windows into your body.
If you open your eyes wide in wonder
and belief, your body fills up with light.

MATTHEW 6:23 MSG

20 ___

....
....
....

20 ___

....
....
....

20 ___

....
....
....

20 ___

....
....
....

20 ___

....
....
....

As we grow in our capacities to see and enjoy the joys that God has placed in our lives, life becomes a glorious experience of discovering His endless wonders.

20___

20___

20___

20___

20___

*Every moment is full of wonder,
and God is always present.*

20 __ ....
....
....
....

20 __ ....
....
....
....

20 __ ....
....
....
....

20 __ ....
....
....
....

20 __ ....
....
....
....

*R*emember that you are needed.
There is at least one important work to be done
that will not be done unless you do it.

CHARLES L. ALLEN

20___ ....
....
....
....

20___ ....
....
....
....

20___ ....
....
....
....

20___ ....
....
....
....

20___ ....
....
....
....

*Joy comes from knowing God loves me
and knows who I am and where I'm going...
that my future is secure as I rest in Him.*

DR. JAMES DOBSON

20 ___ ....
....
....
....

20 ___ ....
....
....
....

20 ___ ....
....
....
....

20 ___ ....
....
....
....

20 ___ ....
....
....
....

I remain confident of this: I will see the goodness
of the LORD in the land of the living. Wait for the LORD;
be strong and take heart and wait for the LORD.

PSALM 27:13–14 NIV

20 _____ ....
....
....
....

20 _____ ....
....
....
....

20 _____ ....
....
....
....

20 _____ ....
....
....
....

20 _____ ....
....
....
....

*W*e may...depend upon God's promises, for...He will be as good as His word. He is so kind that He cannot deceive us, so true that He cannot break His promise.

MATTHEW HENRY

20___

20___

20___

20___

20___

Contentment is not the fulfillment of what you want,
but the realization of how much you already have.

20 __ ....
....
....
....

20 __ ....
....
....
....

20 __ ....
....
....
....

20 __ ....
....
....
....

20 __ ....
....
....
....

Have you ever thought that in every action
of grace in your heart you have the whole
omnipotence of God engaged to bless you?

ANDREW MURRAY

20 ___ ....
....
....
....

20 ___ ....
....
....
....

20 ___ ....
....
....
....

20 ___ ....
....
....
....

20 ___ ....
....
....
....

At every crossroad, follow your dream.
It is courageous to let your heart lead the way.

THOMAS LELAND

20___ ....
....
....

20___ ....
....
....

20___ ....
....
....

20___ ....
....
....

20___ ....
....
....

Be glad for all God is planning for you.
Be patient in trouble, and prayerful always.
ROMANS 12:12 TLB

20___ ....
....
....
....

20___ ....
....
....
....

20___ ....
....
....
....

20___ ....
....
....
....

20___ ....
....
....
....

Never be afraid to trust an unknown future to an all-knowing God.

CORRIE TEN BOOM

20___ ....
....
....
....

20___ ....
....
....
....

20___ ....
....
....
....

20___ ....
....
....
....

20___ ....
....
....
....

*We are truly loving when we help ourselves
and others to be all we are meant to be.*
ALEXANDRA STODDARD

20 __ ....

....

....

20 __ ....

....

....

20 __ ....

....

....

20 __ ....

....

....

20 __ ....

....

....

God puts each fresh morning, each new chance of life, into our hands as a gift to see what we will do with it.

20___ ....
....
....
....
....

20___ ....
....
....
....

20___ ....
....
....
....

20___ ....
....
....
....

20___ ....
....
....
....

*L*ife is what we are alive to. It is not length but breadth....
Be alive to...goodness, kindness, purity, love, history,
poetry, music, flowers, stars, God, and eternal hope.

MALTBIE D. BABCOCK

20 __ ....
....
....
....

20 __ ....
....
....
....

20 __ ....
....
....
....

20 __ ....
....
....
....

20 __ ....
....
....
....

*May the Lord...increase you a thousand
times and bless you as he has promised!*

DEUTERONOMY 1:11 NIV

20___ ....
....
....
....

20___ ....
....
....
....

20___ ....
....
....
....

20___ ....
....
....
....

20___ ....
....
....
....

*Priceless in value, we are handcrafted by God,
who has a personal design and plan for each of us.*
WENDY MOORE

20___ ....
....
....
....

20___ ....
....
....
....

20___ ....
....
....
....

20___ ....
....
....
....

20___ ....
....
....
....

*May our gracious God...meet you
with hope, faith, and strength for whatever
He has placed in front of you to do.*

VALERIE SHEPARD

20___ ....
....
....
....

20___ ....
....
....
....

20___ ....
....
....
....

20___ ....
....
....
....

20___ ....
....
....
....

SEPTEMBER 9

The mind determines what's possible.
The soul surpasses it.

PILAR COOLINTA

20 ___ ....
....
....
....

20 ___ ....
....
....
....

20 ___ ....
....
....
....

20 ___ ....
....
....
....

20 ___ ....
....
....
....

God loves us so much that sometimes He gives us what we need and not what we ask.

MAX LUCADO

20___

....
....
....
....

20___

....
....
....
....

20___

....
....
....
....

20___

....
....
....
....

20___

....
....
....
....

In peace I will lie down and sleep, for you alone,
LORD, make me dwell in safety.

PSALM 4:8 NIV

20___ ....
....
....
....

20___ ....
....
....
....

20___ ....
....
....
....

20___ ....
....
....
....

20___ ....
....
....
....

The future belongs to those who believe
in the beauty of their dreams.

ELEANOR ROOSEVELT

20 __ ....
....
....
....

20 __ ....
....
....
....

20 __ ....
....
....
....

20 __ ....
....
....
....

20 __ ....
....
....
....

All truths are easy to understand
once they are discovered;
the point is to discover them.

GALILEO GALILEI

20___

20___

20___

20___

20___

He is the God of the multitude
and the God of the individual....
He will not overlook your tiniest need.

ROY LESSIN

20___

....

....

....

20___

....

....

....

20___

....

....

....

20___

....

....

....

20___

....

....

....

There is no limit to God's love. It is without measure and its depth cannot be sounded.

MOTHER TERESA

20___ ....
....
....
....

20___ ....
....
....
....

20___ ....
....
....
....

20___ ....
....
....
....

20___ ....
....
....
....

*Keep on asking, and you will receive what you
ask for. Keep on seeking, and you will find.
Keep on knocking, and the door will be opened to you.*

LUKE 11:9 NLT

20___

....

....

....

20___

....

....

....

20___

....

....

....

20___

....

....

....

20___

....

....

....

We are made to reach out beyond our grasp.
OSWALD CHAMBERS

20___ ....
....
....
....

20___ ....
....
....
....

20___ ....
....
....
....

20___ ....
....
....
....

20___ ....
....
....
....

*In the fall, the profusion of colors
makes every leaf a prayer.*
RAYMOND K. PETRUCCI

20___

....
....
....
....

20___

....
....
....
....

20___

....
....
....
....

20___

....
....
....
....

20___

....
....
....
....

God loves us; not because we are lovable
but because He is love, not because He needs
to receive but because He delights to give.

C. S. LEWIS

20___ ....
....
....
....

20___ ....
....
....
....

20___ ....
....
....
....

20___ ....
....
....
....

20___ ....
....
....
....

This is the true joy in life: the being
used for a purpose recognized by yourself
as a mighty one.

GEORGE BERNARD SHAW

20 __ ....
....
....
....

20 __ ....
....
....
....

20 __ ....
....
....
....

20 __ ....
....
....
....

20 __ ....
....
....
....

Wise men and women are always learning,
always listening for fresh insights.
PROVERBS 18:15 MSG

20___ ....
....
....
....

20___ ....
....
....
....

20___ ....
....
....
....

20___ ....
....
....
....

20___ ....
....
....
....

*L*ife is so full of meaning and purpose, so full
of beauty—beneath its covering—that you will
find that earth but cloaks your heaven.

FRA GIOVANNI

20___

....
....
....
....

20___

....
....
....

20___

....
....
....

20___

....
....
....

20___

....
....
....

SEPTEMBER 23

Do not pray for dreams equal to your powers.
Pray for powers equal to your dreams.

ADELAIDE ANN PROCTER

20___ ....
....
....
....

20___ ....
....
....
....

20___ ....
....
....
....

20___ ....
....
....
....

20___ ....
....
....
....

He loves each one of us as if there were only one of us.
AUGUSTINE

20 ___

20 ___

20 ___

20 ___

20 ___

*Each of us, made in [God's] image and likeness,
is yet another promise He has made to the universe
that He will continue to love it and care for it.*

BRENNAN MANNING

20 __ ....
....
....
....

20 __ ....
....
....
....

20 __ ....
....
....
....

20 __ ....
....
....
....

20 __ ....
....
....
....

*F*rom his abundance we have all received
one gracious blessing after another.

JOHN 1:16 NLT

20___

20___

20___

20___

20___

When you were born, God said, "Yes!"

20____

20____

20____

20____

20____

There will be days which are great.... There
will be other days when we aren't sure why we
got out of bed. Regardless...we can be assured
that God takes care of our daily needs.

EMILIE BARNES

20___ ....
....
....
....

20___ ....
....
....
....

20___ ....
....
....
....

20___ ....
....
....
....

20___ ....
....
....
....

Cease to inquire whatever the future has in store,
and take as a gift whatever the day brings forth.

HORACE

20___

20___

20___

20___

20___

We can be assured of this: God, who knows all
and sees all, will set all things straight
in the end. Even better, He will dry every tear.

RICHARD J. FOSTER

20 __ ....
....
....
....

20 __ ....
....
....
....

20 __ ....
....
....
....

20 __ ....
....
....
....

20 __ ....
....
....
....

The LORD your God in your midst,
The Mighty One, will save…
He will quiet you with His love,
He will rejoice over you with singing.

ZEPHANIAH 3:17 NKJV

20 ___ ....
....
....
....

20 ___ ....
....
....
....

20 ___ ....
....
....
....

20 ___ ....
....
....
....

20 ___ ....
....
....
....

There is no rest in the heart of God until He knows that we are at rest in His grace.

LLOYD JOHN OGILVIE

20___ ....
....
....
....

20___ ....
....
....
....

20___ ....
....
....
....

20___ ....
....
....
....

20___ ....
....
....
....

Sunshine spills through autumn-colored leaves, lighting up their brilliance like stained-glass windows in a great cathedral, expressing the wonder of God's love, declaring His glory.

20___ ....
....
....
....

20___ ....
....
....
....

20___ ....
....
....
....

20___ ....
....
....
....

20___ ....
....
....
....

I asked God for all things that I might enjoy life.
He gave me life that I might enjoy all things.

20___ ....
....
....
....

20___ ....
....
....
....

20___ ....
....
....
....

20___ ....
....
....
....

20___ ....
....
....
....

God will never let you be shaken or moved
from your place near His heart.
JONI EARECKSON TADA

20___ ....
....
....
....

20___ ....
....
....
....

20___ ....
....
....
....

20___ ....
....
....
....

20___ ....
....
....
....

Don't worry about anything; instead, pray about everything. Tell God what you need, and thank him for all he has done. Then you will experience God's peace, which exceeds anything we can understand.

PHILIPPIANS 4:6–7 NLT

20___ ....
....
....
....

20___ ....
....
....
....

20___ ....
....
....
....

20___ ....
....
....
....

20___ ....
....
....

We need time to dream, time to remember, and time to reach the infinite. Time to be.

GLADYS TABER

20___ ....
....
....
....

20___ ....
....
....
....

20___ ....
....
....
....

20___ ....
....
....
....

20___ ....
....
....
....

*T*o be alive, to be able to see, to walk, to have a home, music, paintings, friends—it's all a miracle. I have adopted the technique of living life from miracle to miracle.

ARTUR RUBINSTEIN

20___ ....
....
....
....

20___ ....
....
....
....

20___ ....
....
....
....

20___ ....
....
....
....

20___ ....
....
....
....

God's forgiveness and love exist for you as if you were the only person on earth.
CECIL OSBORNE

20___ ....
....
....
....

20___ ....
....
....
....

20___ ....
....
....
....

20___ ....
....
....
....

20___ ....
....
....
....

Nothing we can do will make the Father love us less;
nothing we do can make Him love us more.
He loves us unconditionally with an everlasting love.

NANCIE CARMICHAEL

20 ___ ....
....
....
....

20 ___ ....
....
....
....

20 ___ ....
....
....
....

20 ___ ....
....
....
....

20 ___ ....
....
....
....

*You have made known to me the paths of life;
you will fill me with joy in your presence.*

ACTS 2:28 NIV

20___ ....
....
....
....

20___ ....
....
....
....

20___ ....
....
....
....

20___ ....
....
....
....

20___ ....
....
....
....

*L*ook for the heaven here on earth. It is all around you.

20___

20___

20___

20___

20___

The Lord's goodness surrounds us at every moment. I walk through it almost with difficulty, as through thick grass and flowers.

R. W. BARBER

20___

20___

20___

20___

20___

The uncertainties of the present always give way to the enchanted possibilities of the future.

GELSEY KIRKLAND

20___

_____

_____

_____

20___

_____

_____

_____

20___

_____

_____

_____

20___

_____

_____

_____

20___

_____

_____

_____

*God loves us, and the will of love
is always blessing for its loved ones.*
HANNAH WHITALL SMITH

20___ ....
....
....
....

20___ ....
....
....
....

20___ ....
....
....
....

20___ ....
....
....
....

20___ ....
....
....
....

The LORD is trustworthy in all he promises
and faithful in all he does.... You open your hand
and satisfy the desires of every living thing.

PSALM 145:13, 16 NIV

20___ ....
....
....
....

20___ ....
....
....
....

20___ ....
....
....
....

20___ ....
....
....
....

20___ ....
....
....
....

*E*ach day offers time to draw closer to God
and take new steps toward living with purpose.

20 ___ ....
....
....
....

20 ___ ....
....
....
....

20 ___ ....
....
....
....

20 ___ ....
....
....
....

20 ___ ....
....
....
....

So often in my life...an unexpected burst of golden sunshine has exploded through a black cloud, sending inspiring shafts of warm, beautiful sunshine into my life.

ROBERT SCHULLER

20___ ....
....
....
....

20___ ....
....
....
....

20___ ....
....
....
....

20___ ....
....
....
....

20___ ....
....
....
....

One way to get the most out of life
is to look upon it as an adventure.
WILLIAM FEATHER

20___ ....

20___ ....

20___ ....

20___ ....

20___ ....

The stars exist that we might know
how high our dreams can soar.

20 __ ....

....

....

....

20 __ ....

....

....

....

20 __ ....

....

....

....

20 __ ....

....

....

....

20 __ ....

....

....

....

You will search again for the Lord
your God. And if you search for him with
all your heart and soul, you will find him.

DEUTERONOMY 4:29 NLT

20___ ....
....
....
....

20___ ....
....
....
....

20___ ....
....
....
....

20___ ....
....
....
....

20___ ....
....
....
....

God walks with us.... He scoops us up in His arms or simply sits with us in silent strength until we cannot avoid the awesome recognition that yes, even now, He is there.

GLORIA GAITHER

20 __ ....
....
....
....

20 __ ....
....
....
....

20 __ ....
....
....
....

20 __ ....
....
....

20 __ ....
....
....
....

Each day can be the beginning of a wonderful future.

20___ ....
....
....
....

20___ ....
....
....
....

20___ ....
....
....
....

20___ ....
....
....
....

20___ ....
....
....
....

Just as there comes a warm sunbeam into every cottage window, so comes a love—born of God's care for every separate need.

NATHANIEL HAWTHORNE

20 __ ....

....

....

....

20 __ ....

....

....

....

20 __ ....

....

....

....

20 __ ....

....

....

....

20 __ ....

....

....

....

*Not what we have but what we enjoy
constitutes our abundance.*
JOHN PETIT-SENN

20 ___ ....

....

....

....

20 ___ ....

....

....

....

20 ___ ....

....

....

....

20 ___ ....

....

....

....

20 ___ ....

....

....

....

May you be blessed by the LORD,
the Maker of heaven and earth.

PSALM 115:15 NIV

20___ ....
....
....
....

20___ ....
....
....
....

20___ ....
....
....
....

20___ ....
....
....
....

20___ ....
....
....
....

All the things in this world are gifts and signs of God's love to us. The whole world is a love letter from God.

PETER KREEFT

20___ ....
....
....
....

20___ ....
....
....
....

20___ ....
....
....
....

20___ ....
....
....
....

20___ ....
....
....
....

*God's fingers can touch nothing but
to mold it into loveliness.*

GEORGE MACDONALD

20____ ....
....
....
....

20____ ....
....
....
....

20____ ....
....
....
....

20____ ....
....
....
....

20____ ....
....
....
....

*A dream becomes a goal when action
is taken toward its achievement.*
BO BENNETT

20___ ....
....
....
....

20___ ....
....
....
....

20___ ....
....
....
....

20___ ....
....
....
....

20___ ....
....
....
....

Everybody can be great...because anybody can serve.
You don't have to have a college degree to serve.... You
only need a heart full of grace. A soul generated by love.

MARTIN LUTHER KING JR.

20___

_____

_____

_____

20___

_____

_____

_____

20___

_____

_____

_____

20___

_____

_____

_____

20___

_____

_____

_____

The LORD will work out his plans for my life—
for your faithful love, O LORD, endures forever.

PSALM 138:8 NLT

20___ ....
....
....
....

20___ ....
....
....
....

20___ ....
....
....
....

20___ ....
....
....
....

20___ ....
....
....
....

God loves and cares for us,
even to the least event and smallest need of life.

HENRY EDWARD MANNING

20___ ....
....
....
....

20___ ....
....
....
....

20___ ....
....
....
....

20___ ....
....
....
....

20___ ....
....
....
....

God is every moment totally aware of each one of us.
Totally aware in intense concentration and love.

EUGENIA PRICE

20___ ....

....

....

....

20___ ....

....

....

....

20___ ....

....

....

....

20___ ....

....

....

....

20___ ....

....

....

....

Shoot for the moon. Even if you miss,
you'll land among the stars.

LES BROWN

20___

20___

20___

20___

20___

God is constantly taking knowledge of me in love and watching over me for my good.

J. I. PACKER

20___

20___

20___

20___

20___

God has given each of you a gift from his great variety of spiritual gifts. Use them well to serve one another.

1 PETER 4:10 NLT

20___ ....
....
....
....
....

20___ ....
....
....
....
....

20___ ....
....
....
....
....

20___ ....
....
....
....
....

20___ ....
....
....
....

*The treasure our heart searches for
is found in the ocean of God's love.*

JANET L. SMITH

20___ ....
....
....

20___ ....
....
....

20___ ....
....
....

20___ ....
....
....

20___ ....
....
....

NOVEMBER 7

*Far away, there in the sunshine, are my
highest aspirations. I may not reach them,
but I can look up and see their beauty, believe in them,
and try to follow where they lead.*

LOUISA MAY ALCOTT

20___ ....

20___ ....

20___ ....

20___ ....

20___ ....

The purpose of life is a life of purpose.

ROBERT BYRNE

20___

20___

20___

20___

20___

We have been in God's thought from all eternity,
and in His creative love, His attention never leaves us.

MICHAEL QUOIST

20___ ....
....
....
....

20___ ....
....
....
....

20___ ....
....
....
....

20___ ....
....
....
....

20___ ....
....
....
....

*The Lord has done great things for
us, and we are filled with joy.*

PSALM 126:3 NIV

20___ ....
....
....
....

20___ ....
....
....
....

20___ ....
....
....
....

20___ ....
....
....
....

20___ ....
....
....
....

NOVEMBER 11

*The private and personal blessings we enjoy,
the blessings of immunity, safeguard, liberty, and
integrity, deserve the thanksgiving of a whole life.*

JEREMY TAYLOR

20___ ....
....
....
....

20___ ....
....
....
....

20___ ....
....
....
....

20___ ....
....
....
....

20___ ....
....
....
....

*L*ord...teach me to live this moment only, looking neither to the past with regret, nor the future with apprehension. Let love be my aim and my life a prayer.

ROSEANN ALEXANDER-ISHAM

20 ___ ....

....

....

....

20 ___ ....

....

....

....

20 ___ ....

....

....

....

20 ___ ....

....

....

....

20 ___ ....

....

....

....

Everything God does is love—
even when we do not understand Him.
BASILEA SCHLINK

20___ ....
....
....
....

20___ ....
....
....
....

20___ ....
....
....
....

20___ ....
....
....
....

20___ ....
....
....
....

*F*or God is, indeed, a wonderful Father who longs
to pour out His mercy upon us, and whose majesty
is so great that He can transform us from deep within.

TERESA OF AVILA

20___

....

....

....

20___

....

....

....

20___

....

....

....

20___

....

....

....

20___

....

....

....

Our God gives you everything you need,
makes you everything you're to be.

2 THESSALONIANS 1:2 MSG

20___ ....
....
....
....

20___ ....
....
....
....

20___ ....
....
....
....

20___ ....
....
....
....

20___ ....
....
....
....

*May the God of love and peace set your heart
at rest and speed you on your journey.*
RAYMOND OF PENYAFORT

20___ ....
....
....
....

20___ ....
....
....
....

20___ ....
....
....
....

20___ ....
....
....
....

20___ ....
....
....
....

The goodness of God is infinitely more wonderful
than we will ever be able to comprehend.
A. W. TOZER

20___ ....
....
....
....

20___ ....
....
....
....

20___ ....
....
....
....

20___ ....
....
....
....

20___ ....
....
....
....

*E*ach day is a treasure box of gifts from God just
waiting to be opened. Open your gifts with excitement.
You will find forgiveness attached to ribbons of joy.
You will find love wrapped in sparkling gems.

JOAN CLAYTON

20 __

20 __

20 __

20 __

20 __

*G*od gives us dreams a size too big so
that we can grow in them.

20 __ ....
....
....
....

20 __ ....
....
....
....

20 __ ....
....
....
....

20 __ ....
....
....
....

20 __ ....
....
....
....

Give thanks to the LORD, for he is good!
His faithful love endures forever.

PSALM 106:1 NLT

20 ___ ....
....
....
....

20 ___ ....
....
....
....

20 ___ ....
....
....
....

20 ___ ....
....
....
....

20 ___ ....
....
....
....

Among God's best gifts to us are the people who love us.

20___ ....
....
....
....

20___ ....
....
....
....

20___ ....
....
....
....

20___ ....
....
....
....

20___ ....
....
....
....

You have given so much to me,
Give one thing more—a grateful heart.
GEORGE HERBERT

20 ___ ....
....
....
....

20 ___ ....
....
....
....

20 ___ ....
....
....
....

20 ___ ....
....
....
....

20 ___ ....
....
....
....

Seeing our Father in everything makes life one
long thanksgiving and gives a rest of heart.
HANNAH WHITALL SMITH

20 __ ....
....
....
....

20 __ ....
....
....
....

20 __ ....
....
....
....

20 __ ....
....
....
....

20 __ ....
....
....
....

Thanksgiving puts power in living, because it opens
the generators of the heart to respond gratefully,
to receive joyfully, and to react creatively.

20 ___ ....
....
....
....

20 ___ ....
....
....
....

20 ___ ....
....
....
....

20 ___ ....
....
....
....

20 ___ ....
....
....
....

*R*ejoice always, pray without ceasing,
in everything give thanks.

1 THESSALONIANS 5:16–18 NKJV

20___ ....
....
....
....

20___ ....
....
....
....

20___ ....
....
....
....

20___ ....
....
....
....

20___ ....
....
....
....

To be grateful is to recognize the Love
of God in everything He has given us—
and He has given us everything.

THOMAS MERTON

20 __ ....
....
....
....

20 __ ....
....
....
....

20 __ ....
....
....
....

20 __ ....
....
....
....

20 __ ....
....
....
....

Thanksgiving is a time of quiet reflection upon the past and an annual reminder that God has, again, been ever so faithful.

CHARLES SWINDOLL

20____ ....
....
....
....

20____ ....
....
....
....

20____ ....
....
....
....

20____ ....
....
....
....

20____ ....
....
....

NOVEMBER 28

*W*ere there no God we would be in this glorious
world with grateful hearts and no one to thank.

CHRISTINA ROSSETTI

20＿ ....
....
....
....

20＿ ....
....
....
....

20＿ ....
....
....
....

20＿ ....
....
....
....

20＿ ....
....
....
....

*Joy is the holy fire that keeps our purpose
warm and our intelligence aglow.*

HELEN KELLER

20___

20___

20___

20___

20___

We all live off his generous bounty, gift after gift after gift...this exuberant giving and receiving, this endless knowing and understanding—all this came through Jesus.

JOHN 1:16–17 MSG

20___ ....
....
....
....

20___ ....
....
....
....

20___ ....
....
....
....

20___ ....
....
....
....

20___ ....
....
....
....

*W*isdom is the power to see, and the inclination
to choose, the best and highest goal, together
with the surest means of attaining it.

J. I. PACKER

20 ___ ....

....

....

....

20 ___ ....

....

....

....

20 ___ ....

....

....

....

20 ___ ....

....

....

20 ___ ....

....

....

....

May you grow to be as beautiful as God meant
you to be when He first thought of you.

20___ ....
....
....
....

20___ ....
....
....
....

20___ ....
....
....
....

20___ ....
....
....
....

20___ ....
....
....
....

Walk each day in the simplicity of trusting God's love
and the wonder of watching Him work in marvelous ways.

ROY LESSIN

20___ ....
....
....
....

20___ ....
....
....
....

20___ ....
....
....
....

20___ ....
....
....
....

20___ ....
....
....
....

This love of God is nothing less than the life of God poured out lavishly and constantly.

W. PHILLIP KELLER

20 —— ....
....
....

20 —— ....
....
....

20 —— ....
....
....

20 —— ....
....
....

20 —— ....
....
....

Give generously, for your gifts will return to you later.

ECCLESIASTES 11:1 TLB

20___

_____

_____

_____

_____

20___

_____

_____

_____

20___

_____

_____

_____

20___

_____

_____

_____

20___

_____

_____

_____

Focus your full attention on the goodness and greatness
of your Father rather than on the size of your need.
Your need is so small compared to His ability to meet it.

20 ___ ....
....
....
....

20 ___ ....
....
....
....

20 ___ ....
....
....
....

20 ___ ....
....
....
....

20 ___ ....
....
....
....

*Y*ou pay God a compliment by
asking great things of Him.

TERESA OF AVILA

20___ ....
....
....
....

20___ ....
....
....
....

20___ ....
....
....
....

20___ ....
....
....
....

20___ ....
....
....
....

*A*ll this beauty exists so you and I can see
His glory, His artwork. It's like an invitation
to worship Him, to know Him.

DONALD MILLER

20___ ....

....

....

....

20___ ....

....

....

....

20___ ....

....

....

....

20___ ....

....

....

....

20___ ....

....

....

....

*T*uck [this] thought into your heart today.
Treasure it. Your Father God cares about your
daily everythings that concern you.

KAY ARTHUR

20___

20___

20___

20___

20___

*T*hanks be to God for his indescribable gift!

2 CORINTHIANS 9:15 NIV

20 ___ ....
....
....

20 ___ ....
....
....

20 ___ ....
....
....

20 ___ ....
....
....

20 ___ ....
....
....

The magical dust of Christmas glittered on the cheeks
of humanity ever so briefly, reminding us of what
is worth having and what we were intended to be.

MAX LUCADO

20 __ ....

20 __ ....

20 __ ....

20 __ ....

20 __ ....

DECEMBER 12

You are the ordinary, becoming the extraordinary, all due to Him.

E. STANLEY JONES

20___ ....
....
....
....

20___ ....
....
....
....

20___ ....
....
....
....

20___ ....
....
....
....

20___ ....
....
....
....

*Faith makes the uplook good, the outlook bright,
the inlook favorable, and the future glorious.*
V. RAYMOND EDMAN

20___ ....
....
....
....

20___ ....
....
....
....

20___ ....
....
....
....

20___ ....
....
....
....

20___ ....
....
....
....

*M*ay you wake each day with His blessings
and sleep each night in His keeping.
And may you always walk in His tender care.

20___ ....
....
....
....

20___ ....
....
....
....

20___ ....
....
....
....

20___ ....
....
....
....

20___ ....
....
....
....

The mercy of our God is very tender,
and heaven's dawn is about to break upon us,
to give light...and to guide us to the path of peace.

LUKE 1:78–79 TLB

20 __ ....
....
....
....

20 __ ....
....
....
....

20 __ ....
....
....
....

20 __ ....
....
....
....

20 __ ....
....
....
....

I think miracles exist in part as gifts and in part as clues
that there is something beyond the flat world we see.

PEGGY NOONAN

20 __ ....

....

....

....

20 __ ....

....

....

....

20 __ ....

....

....

....

20 __ ....

....

....

....

20 __ ....

....

....

....

Peace is not a season; it is a way of life.

20___ ....
....
....
....

20___ ....
....
....
....

20___ ....
....
....
....

20___ ....
....
....
....

20___ ....
....
....
....

DECEMBER 18

Today is unique!... At midnight it will end, quietly, suddenly, totally. Forever. But the hours between now and then are opportunities with eternal possibilities.

CHARLES SWINDOLL

20 __ ....
....
....
....

20 __ ....
....
....
....

20 __ ....
....
....
....

20 __ ....
....
....
....

20 __ ....
....
....
....

DECEMBER 19

*The joy of brightening other lives, bearing
each other's burdens, easing others' loads,
and supplanting empty hearts...with generous
gifts becomes for us the magic of Christmas.*

W. C. JONES

20____ ....
....
....
....

20____ ....
....
....
....

20____ ....
....
....
....

20____ ....
....
....
....

20____ ....
....
....
....

*For unto us a Child is born, unto us a Son is given....
And His name will be called Wonderful, Counselor,
Mighty God, Everlasting Father, Prince of Peace.*

ISAIAH 9:6 NKJV

20____ ....
....
....
....

20____ ....
....
....
....

20____ ....
....
....
....

20____ ....
....
....
....

20____ ....
....
....
....

God possesses infinite knowledge and an awareness
which is uniquely His. At all times...I can realize
that He knows, loves, watches, understands,
and more than that, He has a purpose.

BILLY GRAHAM

20___ ....
....
....
....

20___ ....
....
....
....

20___ ....
....
....
....

20___ ....
....
....
....

20___ ....
....
....
....

God's loving initiative to step into
time and space to restore us to Himself
is still a cause for wonder and praise.

GLORIA GAITHER

20 __ ....
....
....
....

20 __ ....
....
....
....

20 __ ....
....
....
....

20 __ ....
....
....
....

20 __ ....
....
....
....

DECEMBER 23

We expect too much at Christmas. It's got
to be magical. It's got to go right. Feasting.
Fun. The perfect present. All that anticipation.
Take it easy. Love's the thing. The rest is tinsel.

PAM BROWN

20___ ....
....
....
....

20___ ....
....
....
....

20___ ....
....
....
....

20___ ....
....
....
....

20___ ....
....
....
....

Many merry Christmases, many happy New Years.
Unbroken friendships, great accumulations of cheerful
recollections and affections on earth, and heaven for us all.

CHARLES DICKENS

20 ___ ....

....

....

....

20 ___ ....

....

....

....

20 ___ ....

....

....

....

20 ___ ....

....

....

....

20 ___ ....

....

....

....

*B*ehold, the virgin shall be with child, and bear a Son,
and they shall call His name Immanuel...God with us.

MATTHEW 1:23 NKJV

20____ ....
....
....
....

20____ ....
....
....
....

20____ ....
....
....
....

20____ ....
....
....
....

20____ ....
....
....
....

𝔐en and women everywhere sigh on December 26
and say they're glad Christmas is all over for another
year. But it isn't over. "Unto you is born...a Savior."
It's just beginning! And it will go on forever.

EUGENIA PRICE

20___ ....

....

....

....

20___ ....

....

....

....

20___ ....

....

....

....

20___ ....

....

....

....

20___ ....

....

....

....

*Your business is with the present;
leave the future in His hands who will be
sure to do the best, the very best for you.*

PRISCILLA MAURICE

20 ___ ....
....
....
....

20 ___ ....
....
....
....

20 ___ ....
....
....
....

20 ___ ....
....
....
....

20 ___ ....
....
....
....

Stand outside this evening. Look at the stars.
Know that you are special and loved
by the One who created them.

20___ ....
....
....
....

20___ ....
....
....
....

20___ ....
....
....
....

20___ ....
....
....
....

20___ ....
....
....
....

*M*ay the Lord continually bless you with
heaven's blessings as well as with human joys.

PSALM 128:5 TLB

20___ ....
....
....
....

20___ ....
....
....
....

20___ ....
....
....
....

20___ ....
....
....
....

20___ ....
....
....
....

May God's love guide you through the
special plans He has for your life.

20 __ ....

....

....

....

20 __ ....

....

....

....

20 __ ....

....

....

....

20 __ ....

....

....

....

20 __ ....

....

....

....

Now let us welcome the New Year
Full of things that have never been.
RAINER MARIA RILKE

20 __ ....
....
....
....

20 __ ....
....
....
....

20 __ ....
....
....
....

20 __ ....
....
....
....

20 __ ....
....
....
....

Ellie Claire™ Gift & Paper Corp.
Brentwood, TN 37027
EllieClaire.com

For I Know the Plans I Have for You: A Five-Year Keepsake Journal
© 2013 by Ellie Claire™ Gift & Paper Corp.

ISBN 978-1-60936-759-6

Scripture references are from the following sources: The Holy Bible, New
International Version®, NIV®. Copyright © 1973, 1978, 1984, 2011 by Biblica,
Inc.™ Used by permission of Zondervan. All rights reserved worldwide. The Holy
Bible, New King James Version (NKJV). Copyright © 1982 by Thomas Nelson,
Inc. The New American Standard Bible® (NASB), copyright © 1960, 1962, 1963,
1968, 1971, 1972, 1973, 1975, 1977, 1995 by The Lockman Foundation. Used by
permission. The New Revised Standard Version Bible (NRSV), Copyright 1989,
1995, Division of Christian Education of the National Council of the Churches
of Christ in the United States of America. Used by permission. The Holy Bible,
New Living Translation (NLT), copyright 1996, 2004, 2007 by Tyndale House
Foundation. Used by permission of Tyndale House Publishers, Inc., Carol Stream,
Illinois 60188. *The Message* (MSG). Copyright © 1993, 1994, 1995, 1996, 2000,
2001, 2002 by Eugene Peterson. Used by permission of NavPress, Colorado
Springs, CO. *The Living Bible* (TLB) © 1971. Used by permission of Tyndale
House Publishers, Inc., Carol Stream, Illinois 60188. All rights reserved.

Excluding Scripture verses and deity pronouns, in some quotations references
to men and masculine pronouns have been replaced with gender-neutral
or feminine references. Additionally, in some quotations we have carefully
updated verb forms and wording that may distract modern readers.

Compiled by Barbara Farmer.
Cover and interior design by Thinkpen Design | ThinkpenDesign.com.

Ellie Claire Gift & Paper Corp. is an imprint of Worthy Publishing.

Printed in China